Be a SUPER SAVER

Claudia Martin

illustrated by Yekyung Kwon

FRANKLIN WATTS
LONDON • SYDNEY

Franklin Watts
First published in Great Britain in 2023 by Hodder & Stoughton
Copyright © Hodder & Stoughton, 2023

 Produced for Franklin Watts by
White-Thomson Publishing Ltd
www.wtpub.co.uk

Editor: Izzi Howell
Designer: Steve Mead

HB ISBN: 978 1 4451 8613 9
PB ISBN: 978 1 4451 8612 2

MIX
Paper from
responsible sources
FSC
www.fsc.org
FSC® C104740

Franklin Watts
An imprint of
Hachette Children's Group
Part of Hodder & Stoughton
Carmelite House
50 Victoria Embankment
London EC4Y 0DZ

An Hachette UK Company
www.hachettechildrens.co.uk

Printed in China

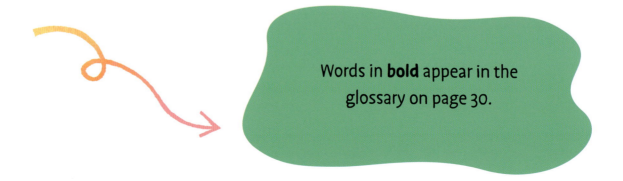

Words in **bold** appear in the glossary on page 30.

CONTENTS

SUPER SAVINGS

Saving is when you do not spend all your money right away. Instead, you put some of it aside to use later. You can save up for a big **purchase** – or you can keep your money safe in case something unexpected and expensive happens in the future.

Spend or save?

If you always spend your money as soon as you get it, you might not be thinking carefully about what you buy. Perhaps you buy a chocolate bar just because it's all you can **afford**. By putting money aside, you can save up to buy things you really need or want, such as a scooter or games console!

Surprise, surprise!

Savings help us prepare for surprises. Savings help adults to meet big, unexpected costs, such as fixing a broken-down car. Usually, young savers have fewer large **expenses**, but savings are useful when you realise you've forgotten to buy your friend a birthday card!

Make it a habit

Saving is a great habit to get into:

☆ Saving can help you afford good-quality items rather than the cheapest ones, which may not last as long.

☆ It helps you cut down on unnecessary purchases.

☆ Savings give you peace of mind because you're more prepared for the unexpected.

☆ Saving helps you achieve your goals, such as taking guitar lessons or visiting a new amusement park!

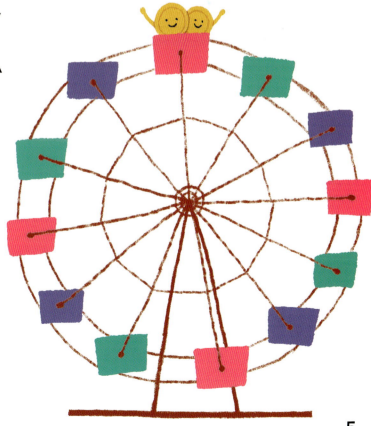

STARTING TO SAVE

How can you start saving? First of all, take a good look at your money. How much money do you have coming in? How much do you regularly spend? You could save the money you have left over!

Income

Your **income** is the money that you receive. Your regular income might be from pocket money and payment for doing chores around the house, for example. Add it all up to find your total income for a week or month.

Weekly income

Pocket money: £1

Payment for washing Mum's car: £2

Payment for cleaning Katy's football boots: 50p

Total: £3.50p

Expenditure

Expenditure is the money that you spend. If you worked out your income for the week or the month, write down your usual expenditure for the same time period.

Weekly expenditure

Magazine: £2.50

Chocolate bar: 60p

Total: £3.10p

Weekly savings

Weekly income: £3.50

Weekly expenditure: £3.10

Money for savings: 40p

Leftovers!

Subtract your expenditure from your income. How much money do you have left over? You could save this money!

MONEY MISSION

Money experts tell us that we should save at least 10 **per cent** of our income. 'Per cent' means 'for every hundred'. This means that, for every £100 you earn, you should save £10. Do you think you can save that much of your income?

NEED OR WANT?

If you want to be a super saver, you need to increase the amount of money you have left over. One way of doing this is to look at your needs and your wants. How much of what you are buying is a want rather than a need?

Needs must

Needs are the things we need to live. We need a home, food, warmth and safety. Wants are things that might make our lives more enjoyable. A coat to keep you warm in winter is a need. But the latest coat from the **brand** everyone's talking about? That's a want.

Wanting more

It can be difficult to tell apart wants and needs, particularly if adults meet our needs without us having to worry about the cost of them! Next time you want to buy something, such as a new games console, ask an adult to help you compare the cost of it with the cost of a need, such as a day's food.

Made a mistake?

Have you ever bought something that you really thought you wanted – but you soon realised you're not going to use it much? Do you wish you had done something else with the money?

MONEY MISSION

A great way to find out how much money you can afford to save is to keep a **journal** of your expenditure. Write a list of everything you buy, then decide which items you could have lived without and which were essential.

GREAT GOALS

It is easier to save if you have a goal. Your goal could be buying something useful for yourself or for someone you love. Another goal could be saving money for a **donation** to your favourite charity.

Short or long?

A short-term goal is something you could achieve within a few weeks, such as buying a book at the end of the month. A long-term goal can be achieved in months or years, such as buying a bike.

Bike

Money I need to save: £80

Weeks to reach goal: 40

Weekly amount to save: £2

Saving plan

Use a notebook to write down the goal you are saving towards. Jot down how much money you need to save. Decide when you want to achieve your goal. Now work out how much you need to save every week.

Be realistic

Make sure your savings goal is realistic. If your weekly pocket money is 50p, you can't save 75p every week! Give yourself more time to reach your goal.

Grown-up goals

Many adults are savers. They save up for big purchases such as Christmas presents, holidays or houses. An even longer-term goal is saving for **retirement**, so they can afford to stop working and still have fun!

TEMPTED?

It is difficult to spend less money when you are being tempted to spend, spend, spend! Temptation comes from advertising, from friends and from wanting that happy buzz when you buy something new.

Ad awareness

Manufacturers create adverts for TV, **social media** and posters that make you feel you need to buy their **products**. Look out for these advertising techniques:

★ Adverts often tell us that our lives will be better if we buy this product. They can do this by showing happy, beautiful people enjoying the product.

★ New films can be linked with branded toys and clothes. If you enjoyed the movie, you might feel the need to buy the products.

★ Social media stars and sportspeople may be paid to wear or talk about products. If you like the star, you can feel drawn to the product.

Peer pressure

Do all your friends have the same cool brand of trainers? It's hard not to want them too! This very common feeling is called **peer pressure**. It is when you feel you have to do something because the people around you – your 'peers' – are doing it.

Think before you buy

With all this temptation, you often need **willpower** to stop yourself making unnecessary purchases. Ask yourself these questions before you spend your money:

☆ Why do I want to buy this product?

☆ How long will this product make me happy?

☆ Is there something else that will make me feel just as happy? How about playing in the park instead of buying a new toy?

SWITCH TO SAVE

There are lots of alternatives to spending your money. Making these switches will help you save money – and you can have fun while you do them, too!

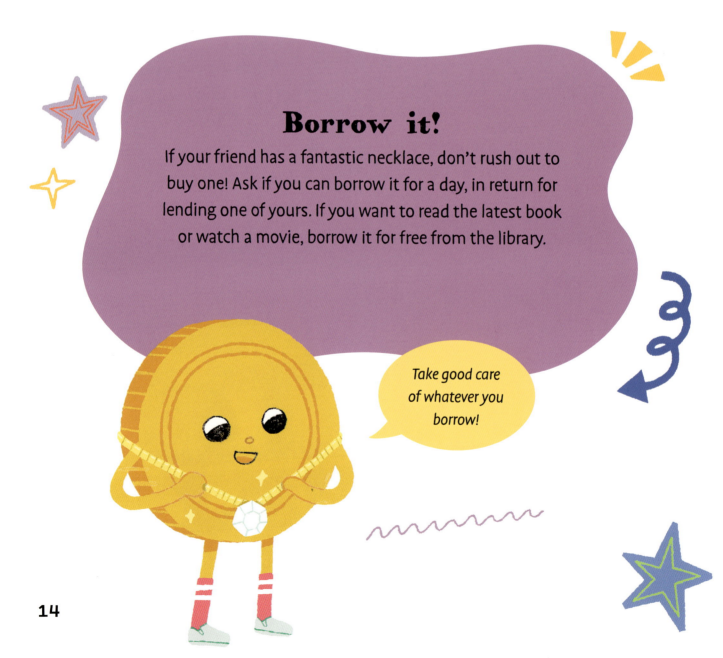

Borrow it!

If your friend has a fantastic necklace, don't rush out to buy one! Ask if you can borrow it for a day, in return for lending one of yours. If you want to read the latest book or watch a movie, borrow it for free from the library.

Take good care of whatever you borrow!

Make it!

Rather than buying branded products from singers or films, make your own fan **merchandise** instead. Draw a comic, film a video or build a model. You will get much more fun from making – and sharing – your creations than from buying anything.

Walk in the woods

Greatest gift

Instead of buying expensive gifts for your family, give them your time. Write 'tokens' for activities they will enjoy doing with you. Tell them they can use their tokens whenever they want.

Watch a film together

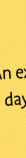

MONEY MISSION

An excellent way to save money is to have a regular no-spend day or week. Choose one day each week, or one week each month, when you will spend no pocket money at all.

MAKE DO

If you really want to save money, make do rather than buy new! Instead of spending money on new clothes and other products, try to repair or reuse what you already have.

Repair

Try to buy new clothes only when you have grown out of the old ones. If clothes are ripped or worn at the knees, ask for an adult's help to mend them. When jeans get too small, you could cut them into shorts.

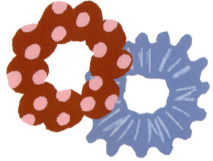

Upcycle

Upcycling is when a used product is recycled into something of higher value. When clothes are too ripped or stained to wear, upcycle them into products you would otherwise buy. You could make hair scrunchies, plaited bracelets or collage greetings cards. Upcycling is better for the environment, too!

If it's not broken ...

Manufacturers often bring out new models of games consoles and phones. The latest games and apps can be used only on new models, which encourages you to buy a new one. Stick with the old one until it breaks! If you've run out of games for your old console, ask an adult for help with swapping games online.

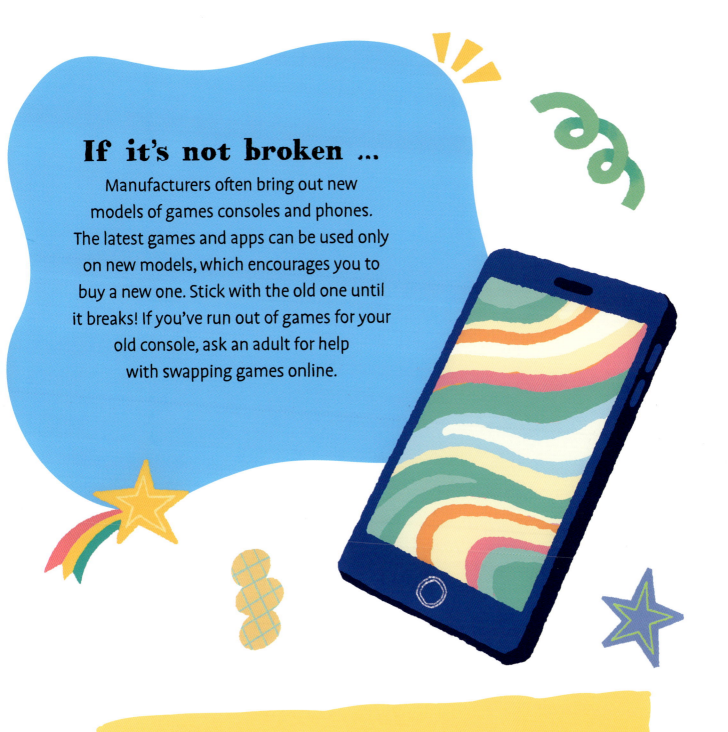

MONEY MISSION

It is easy to waste money on snacks when you're hungry after school or sports. Instead, think ahead! Ask an adult for help with pre-preparing a snack using food you have at home.

STAY MOTIVATED

Saving can be hard work. Sometimes it seems a lot more exciting to spend money on something right now! Try these tips to stay motivated when you're saving.

Eyes on your goal

Keep reminding yourself how important your goal is to you. If you're saving for a football kit, for example, print out a picture of the kit and put it where you can see it. If your goal is a donation to charity, print out a picture of the books, seeds or trees your money will buy.

It all adds up

If you accidentally buy something you didn't plan for, don't just give up on your goal. Do some more sums, adjust your savings plan – and add to your piggy bank when you can.

Stay on track

If you go shopping with friends who always spend lots of money, you might feel pressure to keep up. When they make purchases, don't be embarrassed to explain that you won't because you're saving.

Reward yourself

Split your big savings goal into smaller goals. If you're aiming to save £10, split it into £2.50 goals. When you have saved £2.50, then £5, then £7.50, reward yourself with a sticker or invite a friend over for a sing-along to your favourite musical.

A SAFE PLACE

It is important to keep your savings in a safe place. You could put your money in a piggy bank or, to keep it super safe, you could ask an adult to help you open a **bank account**.

Perfect piggy

A piggy bank is a perfect place to save small amounts of pocket money. Keep your piggy bank in a safe place at home. Never carry all your savings around in a bag or purse, unless you are actually on your way to spend them!

Bank account

A bank account is an arrangement with a **financial** organisation known as a bank. Customers can **deposit** (put in) or **withdraw** (take out) money from their own account. The bank keeps the money safe and keeps a record of what is put in or taken out of the account.

Opening an account

You will need to ask a parent or guardian to set up a bank account for you. Depending on your age and the type of account, an adult may also need to make deposits and withdrawals for you. Older children may be given a bank card, which can be used to withdraw money from a cash machine or pay for purchases in a shop.

MONEY MISSION

Banks are not allowed to lend money to children, so – whether you use a piggy bank or a bank account – you will not be able to withdraw more than you have deposited. Use a journal to keep track of your deposits and withdrawals. Use one column for deposits, one for withdrawals and a third one for your savings total.

GETTING INTEREST

Some bank accounts pay **interest** on savings, which helps your savings to grow little by little. Interest is a small portion of your savings, which the bank adds on to the total every year.

Percentage payments

Interest is worked out as a percentage of your savings. For example, if a bank account pays 1 per cent interest, every year the bank will give you £1 for every £100 you have in the account. This means that if you keep £100 in the account for a year, you will have £101 at the end of the year.

Savings

Interest

Interest rules

Most bank accounts pay low interest or none at all, but usually let you withdraw your money whenever you want. Higher-interest accounts usually have rules, such as saying you must give **notice** before making a withdrawal.

JULY

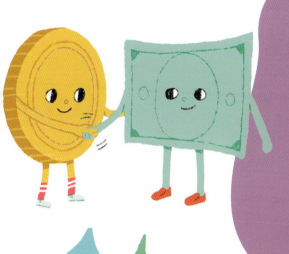

Borrowing

When an adult borrows from a bank, they have to pay the bank interest on the money. Banks usually charge borrowers a bigger percentage of interest than the percentage they pay out to customers. This is one of the ways that banks make money (known as **profit**).

MONEY MISSION

Get to grips with interest by putting 100 toy bricks into a 'bank account'. Your high-interest bank account pays 10 per cent interest, so at the end of the first 'year', give yourself an extra 10 bricks. Now you have 110 bricks. At the end of the second 'year', add interest on your total bricks again: 10 per cent of 110 is 11. Now you have 121 bricks ...

KEEPING IT SAFE

You don't want someone to help themselves to your savings! Never let anyone – except a trusted adult – know the details of your bank account.

Security information

Never write down or share your bank account's **security information** unless a trusted adult says it's OK. Your security information may include:

★ Your bank account number.

★ Your **PIN** (personal identification number) for your bank card, which is the number you type in when you withdraw money or make purchases.

★ Your password for accessing your bank account online.

Don't come any closer!

Card safety

If you have a bank card, never put it in a back pocket or in a bag you leave unattended. When using your card to pay or to withdraw cash, look around to make sure no one is close enough to see your PIN or snatch your cash.

Perfect passwords

Use a different password for each of your accounts. Think up strong passwords that no person or computer program could work out:

☆ Make your passwords at least 12 characters long.

☆ Do not use whole words or number series, such as 1234.

☆ Do use a mix of capital and small letters, numbers, punctuation and symbols, such as ! or %.

☆ Try basing passwords on complicated phrases. For example, the phrase 'My cat Fluffball is 18. Do I cuddle him? Yes!' becomes the password 'McFi18.DIch?Y!'.

SAFE ONLINE

The internet lets us shop without leaving the house. Unfortunately, it also gives criminals a chance to steal our bank security information so they can get rich quick! Always ask an adult for help when shopping online.

Beware phishing

Phishing is when a criminal tries to trick you into giving away your bank security information. They may send an email pretending to be from a bank, with a link to a fake website where you are asked to enter your account details. Remember that your bank and other genuine businesses will never, ever send you an email asking for your personal information.

Watch websites

When shopping online, don't enter your card details until you are sure the website is safe. Check the left-hand side of the address bar has a little padlock, which is usually a sign the site is secure.

Stop malware

Malware is harmful computer programs. Some malware can steal your passwords when you type them in. To avoid downloading malware to your computer or phone, never click on links on websites or in emails until you have checked with an adult.

MONEY MISSION

Check the **balance** (amount of money) in your bank account regularly. If you spot any withdrawals that you haven't made, ask a trusted adult to call your bank's emergency phone line. From the moment you contact the bank, they will stop money being withdrawn.

SO YOU'VE SAVED ...

So now you've reached your savings goal ... Congratulations! Are you ready to spend, spend, spend – or do you need to think, think, think?

Time to think

You have worked hard to save this money, so choose carefully what you spend it on:

★ If you want to buy a product, will it last so you can still use it in a few months or even years?

★ Are you sure that you'll still be excited by this game or fashion trend in a few months' time?

★ Even if you've wanted this purchase for a long time, are you sure it's still the right choice?

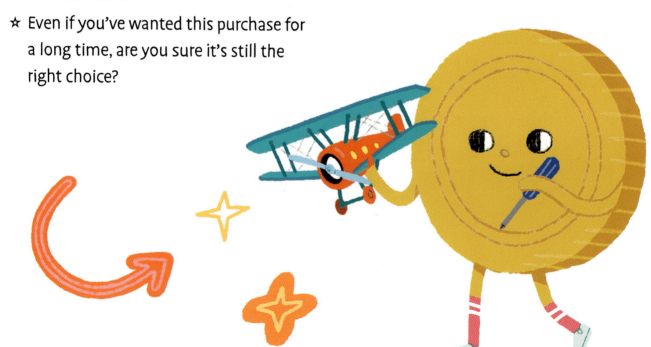

MONEY MISSION

When you've met your savings goal, set yourself a new one! But before you start a new savings journey, write a list of what you've learned so far. Did it take longer than expected to reach your goal? What encouraged you to carry on saving? Has anything you achieved made you feel proud?

Skill for life

You have learned an amazing skill – how to be a super saver! This skill is useful when you are young, but when you are a hard-working, busy adult you will find it very important. Having saving skills helps adults to plan for the future, make smart money choices and meet their goals!

GLOSSARY

afford – to have enough money to pay for something

balance – the amount of money in a bank account

bank account – an arrangement made with a bank that allows a customer to pay in and take out money

brand – a name, symbol or design that a business uses to distinguish its own products from those of other businesses

deposit – to put money in

donation – money or products that are given to charity

expenditure – the amount of money spent

expense – the amount of money used to do or buy something

financial – involved with money

income – all the money someone earns or receives

interest – money paid regularly at a particular rate

journal – a regular written record

manufacturer – a business that makes products for sale

merchandise – things that can be bought and sold

notice – warning of withdrawing money in a certain number of days or weeks

peer pressure – the strong feeling of having to do the same things as other people of the same age or in the same friendship group

per cent – one part of every 100

PIN (personal identification number) – a secret number used with a bank card or to access online banking

product – something that is made to be sold

profit – money that a business has left after it has paid all its expenses

purchase – something that is bought

retirement – when someone stops working because of their age

security information – the secret personal details, numbers and passwords that allow access to a bank account

social media – websites and apps that allow users to share information with each other

willpower – being able to control yourself and not be tempted by unnecessary things

withdraw – to take money out

Books

Economics Made Easy (Super Smart Thinking)
by Jan Miles-Kingston (Wayland, 2021)

Saving Money (Money Box)
by Ben Hubbard (Franklin Watts, 2020)

Super Social Media and Awesome Online Safety
by Clive Gifford (Wayland, 2017)

Websites

natwest.mymoneysense.com/students/students-5-8/keep-helens-money-safe/
Play a game about saving money.

www.bbc.co.uk/bitesize/topics/znvj7yc/articles/z2dsp4j
Find out more about money, saving and budgets.

www.safesearchkids.com/how-to-protect-yourself-against-email-phishing/
Learn all about phishing and how to protect yourself.

INDEX

MASTER YOUR MONEY

TITLES IN THIS SERIES

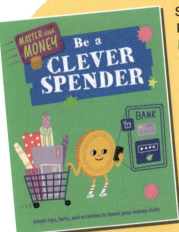

Be a CLEVER SPENDER

Smart tips, facts, and activities to boost your money skills

Sensible spending
Plan ahead
Look at lists
What not to buy
In the mood
Ignore the adverts
Get the best deal!
Size vs cost
Spend to save
Big savings
Better choices
Exciting experiences
The power of money

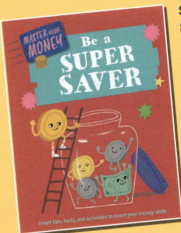

Be a SUPER SAVER

Smart tips, facts, and activities to boost your money skills

Super savings
Starting to save
Need or want?
Great goals
Tempted?
Switch to save
Make do
Stay motivated
A safe place
Getting interest
Keeping it safe
Safe online
So you've saved ...

Know YOUR MONEY

Smart tips, facts, and activities to boost your money skills

Money, money, money
Around the world
Digital dollars
Cryptocurrencies
Making money
Bank basics
Loans
Brainy borrowing
Tax
Rich ...
... and poor
A helping hand
The future of money

Make MEGA MONEY

Smart tips, facts, and activities to boost your money skills

Make money!
Get going
Business basics
Home help
Take care
Make a sale
Excellent events
Crafty business
Write away
Cook it up!
Online artist
Stay safe
Made it!